Top 10 Businesses You Can Successfully Run from Home in 2024-25

The landscape of home-based businesses has evolved significantly, especially in the wake of the global pandemic that began in 2020.

The trend towards remote work and home-based businesses continues to grow, driven by technological advancements and changing attitudes towards work-life balance. Here are ten top businesses that you can successfully run from home in 2024-25.

1. E-commerce Store

Overview

E-commerce remains one of the most viable home-based business opportunities.

With platforms like Shopify, Etsy, and Amazon, anyone can set up an online store to sell products.

Whether it's handmade crafts, vintage items, or dropshipping products, the possibilities are vast.

Key Factors for Success

- Niche Selection:

 Finding a niche market can help you stand out and target a specific audience.

- Quality Products:

 Ensure your products meet high standards to build a loyal customer base.

- Digital Marketing:

 Utilize SEO, social media marketing, and email campaigns to drive traffic to your store.

- Customer Service:

 Providing excellent customer service can lead to repeat business and positive reviews.

Tools and Resources

- E-commerce Platforms:

 Shopify, WooCommerce, Etsy, Amazon.

- Payment Processors:

 PayPal, Stripe, Square.

- Marketing Tools:

 Google Analytics, Mailchimp, Hootsuite.

Challenges

- Competition:

 The e-commerce space is highly competitive.

- Logistics:

 Managing inventory, shipping, and returns can be complex.

2. Freelance Writing and Content Creation

Overview

Freelance writing and content creation remain popular home-based businesses due to the high demand for quality content.

Businesses, blogs, and media outlets constantly need content for their websites, social media, and marketing materials.

Key Factors for Success

- Writing Skills:

 Strong writing skills and the ability to adapt to different styles and formats are crucial.

- Portfolio:

 Building a diverse portfolio can help attract clients.

- Networking:

 Joining freelance platforms and networking with potential clients can lead to consistent work.

Tools and Resources

- Freelance Platforms:

  Upwork, Fiverr, Freelancer.

- Writing Tools:

  Grammarly, Hemingway Editor, Scrivener.

- Content Management Systems:

  WordPress, Medium.

Challenges

- Income Stability:

 Freelancers often face fluctuating income and must manage their finances carefully.

- Time Management:

 Balancing multiple projects and deadlines can be challenging.

3. Virtual Assistance

Overview

Virtual assistants (VAs) provide administrative, technical, or creative assistance to clients remotely.

The rise of remote work has increased the demand for VAs, making it a lucrative home-based business.

Key Factors for Success

- Skillset:

 Proficiency in administrative tasks, communication, and software tools.

- Reliability:

 Being dependable and maintaining a high level of professionalism.

- Client Management:

 Efficiently managing client relationships and expectations.

Tools and Resources

- Project Management Tools:

  Trello, Asana, ClickUp.

- Communication Tools:

  Zoom, Slack, Microsoft Teams.

- Time Tracking Tools:

  Toggl, Clockify.

Challenges

- Client Acquisition:

 Finding and retaining clients can be difficult.

- Work-Life Balance:

 Managing work hours and personal time effectively.

4. Online Tutoring and Teaching

Overview

The demand for online education has surged, creating opportunities for online tutors and teachers.

Whether it's academic subjects, language instruction, or professional skills, online teaching can be a rewarding home-based business.

Key Factors for Success

- Subject Expertise:

 Deep knowledge of the subject you are teaching.

- Teaching Skills:

 Ability to convey information clearly and engage students.

- Platform Selection:

 Choosing the right platform for delivering your lessons.

Tools and Resources

- Teaching Platforms:

 VIPKid, Teachable, Udemy, Coursera.

- Video Conferencing Tools:

 Zoom, Google Meet, Skype.

- Learning Management Systems:

 Moodle, Canvas.

Challenges

- Student Engagement:

 Keeping students motivated and engaged remotely.

- Technical Issues:

 Dealing with technical problems that may arise during online sessions.

5. Social Media Management

Overview

Social media management involves creating, scheduling, and analyzing content for businesses to help them grow their online presence.

With businesses recognizing the power of social media, this field offers great potential for home-based entrepreneurs.

Key Factors for Success

- Understanding Platforms:

 In-depth knowledge of various social media platforms and their algorithms.

- Content Creation:

 Ability to create engaging and relevant content.

- Analytics:

 Using analytics to measure performance and adjust strategies.

Tools and Resources

- Social Media Tools:

 Hootsuite, Buffer, Sprout Social.

- Graphic Design Tools:

 Canva, Adobe Spark.

- Analytics Tools:

 Google Analytics, Facebook Insights.

Challenges

- Keeping Up with Trends:

 Staying updated with the latest trends and platform updates.

- Client Expectations:

 Managing and meeting client expectations can be demanding.

6. Graphic Design

Overview

Graphic design is a versatile field that offers numerous opportunities for home-based businesses.

From logo design and branding to digital illustrations and marketing materials, skilled designers are always in demand.

Key Factors for Success

- Design Skills:

 Proficiency in design software and a strong creative vision.

- Portfolio:

 Building a diverse portfolio showcasing your work.

- Client Communication:

 Effectively communicating with clients to understand their needs and deliver on expectations.

Tools and Resources

- Design Software:

 Adobe Creative Suite (Photoshop, Illustrator, InDesign), Sketch, Figma.

- Portfolio Platforms:

 Behance, Dribbble.

- Freelance Platforms:

 99designs, DesignCrowd.

Challenges

- Competitive Market:

 Standing out in a crowded market can be challenging.

- Client Revisions:

 Handling multiple revisions and client feedback.

7. Digital Marketing Consulting

Overview

Digital marketing consultants help businesses develop and implement effective online marketing strategies.

This can include SEO, PPC, content marketing, email marketing, and more. As businesses continue to focus on their online presence, the demand for digital marketing experts grows.

Key Factors for Success

- Marketing Knowledge:

In-depth understanding of digital marketing channels and strategies.

- Analytical Skills:

Ability to analyze data and adjust strategies accordingly.

- Communication:

Strong communication skills to convey strategies and results to clients.

Tools and Resources

- Marketing Platforms:

 Google Ads, Facebook Ads, Mailchimp.

- SEO Tools:

 SEMrush, Ahrefs, Moz.

- Analytics Tools:

 Google Analytics, Hotjar.

Challenges

- Rapid Changes:

 Keeping up with the fast-paced changes in digital marketing.

- Client Results:

 Ensuring clients see measurable results from their marketing efforts.

8. Affiliate Marketing

Overview

Affiliate marketing involves promoting products or services for other companies and earning a commission on sales generated through your referral links.

It's a performance-based business model that can be highly profitable when done right.

Key Factors for Success

- Niche Selection:

 Choosing a profitable niche that you are passionate about.

- Traffic Generation:

 Driving traffic to your affiliate links through blogs, social media, or paid advertising.

- Content Creation:

 Creating valuable content that promotes affiliate products.

Tools and Resources

- Affiliate Networks:

 Amazon Associates, ShareASale, Commission Junction.

- Content Management Systems:

 WordPress, Blogger.

- Marketing Tools:

 SEMrush, Google Analytics, Mailchimp.

Challenges

- Competition:

 Many niches are highly competitive.

- Income Stability:

 Affiliate income can be inconsistent and dependent on traffic and sales.

9. Subscription Box Service

Overview

Subscription box services have become increasingly popular, offering curated products delivered to customers on a regular basis.

This model can be applied to various niches, including beauty, food, fitness, and more.

Key Factors for Success

- Unique Offering:

 Curating a unique and appealing selection of products.

- Customer Experience:

 Providing an excellent unboxing experience and high-quality products.

- Marketing:

 Using effective marketing strategies to attract and retain subscribers.

Tools and Resources

- E-commerce Platforms:

 Cratejoy, Shopify.

- Payment Processors:

 Stripe, PayPal.

- Marketing Tools:

 Instagram, Facebook Ads,
Influencer Partnerships.

Challenges

- Inventory Management:

 Managing inventory and logistics can be complex.

- Customer Retention:

 Keeping subscribers engaged and reducing churn rates.

10. Online Coaching and Consulting

Overview

Online coaching and consulting encompass various fields, including business, health, fitness, career, and personal development.

Coaches and consultants provide personalized advice and guidance to help clients achieve their goals.

Key Factors for Success

- Expertise:

 Deep knowledge and experience in your coaching or consulting niche.

- Communication Skills:

 Ability to effectively communicate and connect with clients.

- Client Results:

 Delivering measurable results that demonstrate the value of your services.

Tools and Resources

- Coaching Platforms:

  CoachAccountable, BetterUp.

- Communication Tools:

  Zoom, Skype, Google Meet.

- Marketing Tools:

  LinkedIn, Facebook Ads, Content Marketing.

Challenges

- Client Acquisition:

 Finding and retaining clients can be challenging.

- Building Trust:

 Establishing credibility and trust with clients is crucial.

Conclusion

Starting a home-based business in 2024-25 offers numerous opportunities across various industries.

The key to success lies in leveraging your skills and passions, staying updated with industry trends, and utilizing the right tools and resources.

Each business has its own set of challenges, but with dedication and strategic planning, you can build a thriving home-based business that offers flexibility, independence, and financial rewards.

Please use the next few pages for your notes and debates.

www.ingramcontent.com/pod-product-compliance
Lightning Source LLC
Chambersburg PA
CBHW072018230526
45479CB00008B/287